"....If You Have Doubts."

Patty Harris

authorHOUSE®

AuthorHouse™
1663 Liberty Drive, Suite 200
Bloomington, IN 47403
www.authorhouse.com
Phone: 1-800-839-8640

First published by AuthorHouse 7/24/2008

ISBN: 978-1-4343-9722-5 (sc)

Printed in the United States of America
Bloomington, Indiana

This book is printed on acid-free paper.

Dedications

Gary (Whitey) Harris, 1942-2006

My children, my granddaughter Morgan, who has lived so much for her years. I love you all

Special Thanks

My parents, Frank and Connie
(Nardone) Priestas

My Brother, Ray

All my aunts and uncles, for
strength, support and love.

Introduction

This is a true story of my family's struggle and heartbreak dealing with illness and drug addiction. It is not necessarily a spiritual book, however without divine intervention how could these tragedies and miracles have happened? You decide. I know what I think. Why are we still here? What purpose do we have? What can we do with these experiences? I still don't know for sure. However, I have a great desire to share our story. Possibly we can make some other families that have encountered similar situations, know that they are not alone.

I began this as a journal years ago, mainly because I could not say these things aloud and I needed to express myself in some way so I chose to write. This was the only way I could keep this private. It was my way of dealing with the situations that were out of my control. I have been writing for five years and my life has made many changes. Much beyond my belief and there are times I cannot believe that all these past encounters actually happened. I have survived them, where did the strength come from?

1
The Beginning

I was fortunate to have been raised by a very loving, traditional family. My father was of polish decent and my mother was Italian. Born in Italy and arriving in the United States at Ellis Island as a baby in 1919.

My childhood was very average, maybe even a little boring, now that I think about it. My brother and I attended both Public and Catholic schools in the small town where we grew up. My mother still lives there along with many members of her family. It is a unique little town with one store and a post office with no mail delivery. Even today you need to walk to the post office to pick up the mail.

My brother and I grew up very close to our aunts and uncles. We were just one big happy family. Our aunts and uncles were very close to all the nieces and nephews. I remember well the "wiener roasts" we would have at Aunt Rose and Uncle Bill's in their back yard. At a moments notice we would all get together and roast hot dogs after gathering twigs to roast them on the outdoor fireplace the Uncle Bill had made. It was so fun and not a lot of fuss, just simple. All the cousins would provide entertainment by performing their special talents. It seemed as though the accordion was the popular instrument and "Lady of Spain" was the popular song. Not me, I had no special talent, I just went to eat the hot dogs and have fun with my aunts, uncles and cousins. Sundays was also a fun day, we would all meet at Aunt Lena's and Uncle Al's. At that time we were small enough to fit in the kitchen and the children would play in the yard....not possible now, the family has grown to well over 100. On special occasions we now have to rent a hall to get together. Those old days have special memories for me and they will never be forgotten.

Today when we have picnics or get togethers we overdue everything, why do we do that, we make so much work for ourselves and it was just as much fun when we kept it simple. But I guess we will go on doing what we do and we can't go back to the simple life anyway.

My father's family was a little different and we were not quite as close, however, I do have fond memories of my grandfather and the old homestead. Grandpap would play polkas on the fiddle along with the radio and there would be dancing in the kitchen. My grandfather also make homemade beer and root beer. That root beer was a real treat for the children. I remember grandpap pouring a shot of whiskey for the adults. His hands would shake so bad, but he never spilled a drop. It was a lot of fun to spend time with dad's family too. I don't know as much about my father's childhood as I do about my mother's.

My mother tells very sad, but beautiful stories of her childhood and through these stories I can understand the reasons for the closeness she feels for her brothers and sisters and the strong bond they have with one another. One story in particular that she still tells today often, at our request, is about the illness and death of her younger sister, Melina. I like for her to share this story because in today's lifestyle it is difficult to imagine these things . I think we all need to take a step back in time and think about how our ancestors survived their hardships. Just to think that what we consider everyday normal situations were very difficult at that time. Their sister was a young teenager and became very ill and hospitalized. Now this was probably around 1936 or so. There were no major highways and very few family's had automobiles, certainly not this family. The hospital was about 10, 15 miles away from their home. When I asked my mom how they would get there, she would simply say they would try and get a ride or go out in the cold and hitch hike and some one would take them to the hospital. Now she didn't make a big deal of this, she just says it like nothing was wrong with this. If she wanted to see her sister this is simply what she had to do.

But the really sad thing is, when her sister passed away, she tells of how difficult it was to dress her properly for burial. She managed to do it, going to stores and asking for credit for a dress that may have cost $2.00. She still feels guilt over the fact that she had to bury her sister in slippers and not shoes. Can you imagine this? We fret over such minor things today.

Well she has many stories similar to this and when she tells them she really takes you back in time. I love to hear about these stories and so do my children. Since the death of my grandmother Theresa, the family strives diligently to keep tradition and the closeness we all felt years ago. It is a difficult task at times because of the size of the family and life styles of today. Having the annual family reunion and traditional Christmas Eve party is a lot of hard work. My mother is oldest of seven at age 89 and along with her brothers and sisters they try to keep things moving and not let the family traditions die. What will happens when they are gone remains to be seen, I guess we all feel they will be there forever.

I have very fond memories of my school years, both elementary and high school. My brother and I attended Catholic Elementary School and public high school. We had a very solid family life, my father was a steel mill worker and my mother worked at times, but mostly I remember her as a stay at home mom, cooking and cleaning and always doing for us. It was a house that always welcomed family and friends. I always had a lot of activity going on in the house, still do as a matter of fact. I have been very fortunate to remain friends with many of my high school friends. They have always been there for me with their support and love.

2

Finding Love
& Marriage

In the mid 1960's I met Whitey Harris, my life would never be dull again. It was just a casual meeting and we soon became "just" friends. I was not interested in dating him as he was a young man separated and getting a divorce. I liked him but this was just too much for this Catholic Italian to deal with. You see Whitey got married during his senior year in high school and had two children. I guess it wasn't much of a marriage, it was just one of those things. A child was on the way and getting married was the right thing to do.

Anyway we remained "just" friends for a while before we began dating. My parents found out about Whitey's past and didn't want me to see him anymore. That's when we really began dating, figure that. We dated secretly for several years, (maybe not so secretly.)

I struggled with our relationship, as I was not happy with the situation over the religion and the rules of divorce in the Catholic Church, and the fact that I was secretly seeing Whitey. This went against everything I was brought up to believe. The church issue was the biggest. After all, this was a couple that was married very, very young and this divorce would be hanging over there heads for the rest of their lives. I spoke to many priests and no one could help , if we were to marry I would be excommunicated from the catholic church. After trying and being disappointed several times by the answers I would get, and after an encounter with the priest at my hometown church that was extremely difficult I just gave up the idea of ever getting married in a church. The Catholic Church refused to marry us and I couldn't marry in another church so we decided to get married by a justice of the peace. Whitey even went to see my mother and tell her of his intentions, which seemed to help matters. Both of my parents accepted the situation and we dated until August of 1965 when we were married in my parent's living room. It was certainly was not my dream wedding, you know, a church, beautiful wedding gown and lovely reception. It was a Justice of the Peace in my parent's living room. It was not a happy day as I was full of guilt about the church, feeling I would be damned forever for being married outside the church and also that I had disappointed my parents. One thing I felt very strongly about was that I was a good person and if God wanted me to be married in church someday there would be a way. I had to accept things as they were and go on with life.

Well the next few years passed, our marriage was fine but we were always plagued with financial problems, it was just a way of life for us. We struggled with child support, which always came out of Whitey's pay first. We would pay household expenses with what was leftover. Whitey was a steel mill worker so there were also strikes to deal with, but somehow we always seemed to manage at the difficult times. I also worked to help out.

Our first child Gary was born March 3, 1968 and our daughter Rae was born June 14, 1971. Rae was actually born on Whitey's brother Keith's birthday. Keith was killed in an automobile accident when he was sixteen and Whitey was fifteen and present in another car when Keith was killed, how awful it must have been for their family.

My due date for Rae was in June and Whitey had hoped our second child would be born on that day, he got his wish. Rae was born on Keith's birthday.

I would say that both Gary and Rae had a very normal childhood. We tried hard to be good parents and surround them with a good environment. Even though I always worked to help keep our head above water, we stayed very involved with the children. After all there was child support, strikes, layoffs and of course the big steel mill closing at the plant where Whitey and many of our friends worked.

I previously stated that "if we were meant to be married in church God would find a way." Well after fifteen years of being married and living in sin, as the church would say, I received a call from our priest at the church that we attended and were members. Both of the children were baptized Catholic and received the necessary sacraments of the church. The church had done house-to-house survey on active members. When they arrived at my house I answered the questions on the survey and that was that. Several weeks later the priest called and asked me why we had never been married in church and I told him that the church refused to marry us. He wanted to know if we wanted help and he would try and help us receive the marriage sacrament in the church. I really didn't know what to say, this had to be up to Whitey as he was the one that was married before not me. I had no idea what his reaction would be and how he would handle going through Catholic Tribunal for and annulment. After all we had already been married fifteen years and were raising our children living as Catholics with the exception that I was unable to receive the sacrament of communion. We were pretty settled the way things were. I had mixed emotions about the whole ordeal. When I wanted help no one could or would help. Why now? At this stage of our marriage we were having ups and downs like all couples do and I wasn't sure I wanted to be married at all and this surprise comes along.

When Whitey came home from work that day, I told him the phone call and explained to him that if he didn't want to go through with this he didn't have to, but if he started the process he needed to finish it and it would be something he would have to do on his own. He said yes, he would do this for me so I would be able to receive communion that I had not received for fifteen years. The process took one year and one hundred dollars. He also had to involve two people that knew him way back when.

The procedure took place and we were finally married in the church. Oddly enough the annulment was granted on the August 20, our original anniversary date. We'll this was what I wanted, not necessarily fifteen years later but the mere fact that the opportunity fell in our laps and he was so willing to do this for me was a true sign that it was meant to be and so it was. We would continue to make the best of our marriage and go one with our life as it was.

We were very involved in sports with the children. Whitey coached little league and football and I sponsored the cheerleaders. I would say we were a typical American family.

When Gary was a senior in high school is around the time the mill closed and it was a difficult time, we almost lost our home, but managed to save it and Gary did go on to college, with the help of a home equity and student loans.

Rae's high school year seemed to be okay, she stayed active also. There were disappointments but she seemed to handle them. Now I'm not so sure she did as well as she let us believe.

Gary was much easier to raise than Rae, you know all the girl stuff to deal with. Gary really never caused me any trouble. However I always had this funny feeling about Gary and that he was going to cause me heartbreak. I couldn't put my finger on it but the feeling was always there.

Rae seemed to be on the right track, she just always had a tremendous desire to please her friends. Which would later get her into a lot of trouble. The older she got the worse it became.

She had worked as a lifeguard at the local swimming pool during high school and she seemed to be happy. After high school and a few semesters in college, she got a job at our local hospital where I was also working. She took classes at Community college and as time went on she got a better full time job at the hospital. She bought her own car and even though she was still at home she was on her own financially. Things were looking up.

Gary almost completed college, with only another semester left, he did not go back. He was working full time and was on his own financially also. He even bought my father's apartment building and moved into one of the apartments.

Finally, could this be? Whitey and I can breath, Whitey was back to work and I got a better job at the hospital.

I still had these funny feelings about Gary, I guess you can call it mother's intuition. Something is

not right with Gary. In the back of my mind....
drugs...drugs....drugs. I couldn't shake the
feeling. I would confront him often, as I am not
one to hide my thoughts. He would assure me
everything was okay and I would try and block
out the thoughts. I had no real evidence; he was
paying his bills and going to work everyday, so I
would find comfort in this. I would just pray that
I was wrong and this feeling was paranoia and
it would go away. All I wanted was for Gary to
find a nice girl and settle down to raise a family.
I remember very clearly on night Whitey and I
were on a trip and I awakened on morning with
the thoughts of bad dream I had that night, it was
about Gary and drugs. I didn't say anything to
Whitey. When he awakened he said that he had a
bad dream about Gary and drugs. What was this
all about, we both had the same dream? I told
him that I also had a dream like this. This was
really freaky and stayed with me for quit a while.
I don't even remember now if we ever mentioned
it again. After all it was just a dream.

3
Gary's Addiction

As I have previously stated Gary never really caused me problems other that the normal boy things. He was the first grandchild on my side so he always got plenty of love and attention everywhere we went. He played with all the normal boy toys, trucks, bikes, etc. Enjoyed sports, playing baseball and football. Even though Whitey was his coach he never got pressured by his father.. We both tried very hard not to be the type of parents that put to much pressure on the children. I still don't know if we succeeded.

Gary always had a lot of friends and a great sense of humor, both in grade school, high school and college. Now I'm not saying he didn't get into mischief, he did, things like throwing snowballs at moving cars....having parties every time we went away and as I had later found out, much, much more.

One day, during his college years, Whitey found a bag of money and marijuana Gary left setting out, by mistake I'm sure. Whitey went crazy, called me at work and I came home immediately to deal with this. We confronted him and he told us some story that this was not his and who it belonged to. We gave him the benefit of doubt and told him to get this out of our house and he did as far as we know. And believe me I didn't believe him.

This incident secured the seed in my mind that had been there for many years and it continued to grow. He was always confronted and he would tell some story that we half believed or wanted to believe. He went back to college with his friends and continued doing whatever he was doing. I knew he was partying a lot, by the fall in his grades. He was barely getting by. We continued helping him financially as long as we could. I really wanted him to get a college education. Gary came home for the summers and worked at various jobs, it seemed as though he was trying and this is all we expected

By his 4th year money was tight and his grades were not so good. We just couldn't help him anymore, especially if he was not making an effort to keep his grades up. He didn't fight us on this decision and came home. Maybe this was one of those situations that a college education meant more to me than it meant to him. I remember telling him how bad I felt when his two best friends were graduating from college and I felt he should have been there with them. He just told me not to feel bad, he didn't.

Well time passed he was working full time and doing well. He bought a car paid his own bills and didn't require any help from us. It seemed that he was heading in the right direction. Still suspicious about certain things, I would tell myself he was fine, even though I had this bad feeling.

About the apartment building! My father owned an apartment building next door to their home and wanted to sell it. I thought it would be a good investment for Gary and told him so, at first he didn't seem interested, then one day he said "I'm going to buy pap's building." I was happy, but surprised, I wondered why all of sudden he was so anxious to move out of the house. It was time for him to be on his own and I knew that, but the suspicious side of me wanted to know why the rush. Well it happened, he bought the building, did lots of work in it and moved into one of the apartments. Gary seemed happy and my dad was happy and proud. My dad and Gary were very close and he really wanted Gary to have this.

Again everything seemed to be okay. We saw him often; he went to work and paid his bills. Mom and Dad lived right next so they would see him often also. They had a very close relationship. Even though he seemed to be doing all the right things and being where he was supposed to be I was still very suspicious. Maybe all of the feeling I was having was because I am a bit of a control freak and my son is out on his own and I can't handle it!!

Well soon things began to change, most of Gary's friends got married and he was spending less time with them and more time with some new friends. Of course I didn't like that. I wasn't happy with his new friends and he began changing. We would see him less and he began missing work, sleeping until all hours of the day. I knew in my gut what was going on. I would confront him about my suspicions, it did no good. He was changing in every way and I couldn't do a thing to help him. During this time his grandfather passed away and his father had become ill. Whitey was suffering with lung disease. His sister had a child. Things were certainly changing and Gary was turning into some person that I didn't know. He told us that he was leaving his job to go into business for himself. I knew he had the talent to go on his own, but I felt sure he didn't have the self discipline to conduct his own business. That became apparently clear soon, he would get jobs and not show up or I would get phone calls from clients looking for him. This would just verify my suspicions that he was definitely involved in drugs.

At one point Whitey was in the hospital. When Rae and I decided it was time for some intervention. We met at our home to try and discuss what we suspected....drugs were definitely involved and he didn't deny it. He almost couldn't, he had received notice he was losing the building and his vehicle. He agreed he was sinking and couldn't sink much lower. I felt good about our meeting and felt that all this would knock some sense into his head and maybe it did for a while. I'm not sure.

We all felt very badly over the building, as it belonged to my father and I so wanted Gary to have it. Oh well, it wasn't to be. Soon Gary moved in with Rae, as he didn't want to come home. At this point he wasn't employed and tried to do some side jobs, again it seemed like he was trying and we gave him the benefit of doubt. He gradually lost all interest in working but seemed to be available when we needed him. He was very helpful with the care of his niece and he and

Rae seemed to get along fine. Again I still was suspicious of everything but thought maybe he learned a lesson from our disappointment over the loss of the building etc. I was very confused about all of this, and what to do about it. There is not an easy way to explain how I felt. Maybe it is all because we love our children so much we can't see the truth, or don't want to, even though deep down in our hearts we do know the truth.

Gary and Rae soon moved into a small house Rae rented from her stepsister. There was more room and a yard, it seemed to be a good idea at the time...wrong again...!! I should have minded my own business instead of encouraging this move. It was a disaster. Gary was not working, Rae who seemed like the responsible one, began missing work and they couldn't pay rent. I helped as much as I could for my granddaughter's sake, but it financially became impossible.

Whitey's health became more serious and we felt it necessary to get him out the cold weather, he was now on oxygen 24 hours a day. Friends of ours told us of an inexpensive condo village in Florida. We checked it out and bought a condo for the winter months. That was the plan anyway. I was still working and was not quite ready to give up my paycheck. We soon realized the expense of having two homes was not in our budget. We put our home on the market and planned to make Florida our home. Our home, which we had built and I thought it would be the family household forever. I thought wrong. Leaving my home was hard and selling all my stuff was also difficult. We had no choice. Another episode of pneumonia for Whitey would be much too serious for his lung condition.

My kids are in a mess, my husband is very ill, my father had recently passed and I was going to sell my house and belongings. I was going to leave my hometown, my job and my 81 year old mother, who needs me more now that ever. Talk about quilt!!!!

After a year on the market, we sold our home that I thought would be ours until death. We sold or gave away everything. It would be too difficult and expensive to move everything so we said goodbye to all of our cherished possessions. This didn't seem to bother Whitey as much as it did me; I guess women are much more attached to material things than men. I felt like I was abandoning my family especially my granddaughter and my mother, but I felt my duty was to go with my husband for health reasons. I could only pray that the children would turn their life around and decide to follow. After a lot of thought we decided to buy an inexpensive house in PA, so that I would be sure that my granddaughter would have a home and beside it would be a place for us to come home to when we would visit. Seemed like a good idea at the time….wrong again!!!!

There wasn't much money left after the sell of the house, there was a home equity loan to be paid off, a nice down payment on the house we were buying and then paying back the money we had borrowed to buy the condo in Florida. It was agreed that the children would pay us rent for the mortgage. Well I was patient for two years waiting for something that never happened. I know what you are thinking, along with my family and friends, why didn't I throw them out??…Much easier said than done. I just kept getting promises and believed that I would soon be getting money. It just never happened. If I would throw them out what would happen to Morgan? I couldn't do it. They even had some, so called "friends" stay there, this really upset me. Now even these "friends" were living in my house rent-free. I kept saying they have to move out and was told it was only until they found a place to live. This was getting worse the only good thing was Morgan seemed happy. I was stuck in Florida with a sick husband.

I would make many trips home during these years to check on them and Morgan. This would only make my credit cards go sky high. What money that was left from the sell of the house soon vanished and we were just about broke. A lot of good it did, everything just kept getting worse and we were all miserable.

My mother had major surgery during this time and I would try to be there during these times leaving Whitey home alone. However he never made it hard for me to leave and go home, he knew how I felt and agreed that I should be with my mother and would have gone with me if possible. Traveling had become difficult for him and besides one ticket to PA to cheaper than two. Whitey also had a friend, Charlie, who was a retired pilot and offered me buddy passes that helped. Then one day on the plane I was sitting next to a guy and we began talking, this man was also a pilot, on his way home for Thanksgiving. It's really funny how things happen, he obviously could see pain on my face and in my eyes as we conversed. Every trip home was full of sadness, anger and worry it was never a happy situation. Any way this wonderful man named Tony offer me buddy passes whenever I needed one and I actually did use one or two. I still receive a Christmas cards from him, thank you so much Tony. I will never forget you.

On these trips home I would continuously confront the kids about my suspicions of drugs and they would talk their way out of things and I would again give them the benefit of doubt and heard what I wanted to hear. I never believed their stories, but there seemed to be nothing I could do. When I would go home to see them, I would even be confronted by their neighbors and they would tell me that I better take care of the situation at the house. I guess there would be people going in and out, all the time and things were very suspicious. I immediately would go inside and told them of the confrontation and as usual they would talk themselves out of the predicament. I knew the insinuations were correct but chose to believe whatever they would tell me. I really didn't know what I could do. This was a mess and totally out of my control. There was never piece of mind, either when I was back in Pa. or with Whitey in Florida. With his health, as it was, I tried to keep most of these things from him. Now all I could do is pray as I tried to put them in God's hands. This was difficult, being a bit of a control person myself, I was failing with them.

I would bring Morgan to spend time with us in Florida when I could and Rae would come and spend the Christmas with us several years. When Morgan would spend time with us in Florida was the only time I had piece of mind for her. She was like my third child, and my reason for everything.

Morgan spent a lot of time with Whitey and I, after all the first three years of her life Rae and Morgan lived with us. When Whitey's health worsened Rae and Morgan moved into their own place.

Gary would just not come to visit and said he never would.

I could see him drifting away and Rae slipping further into depression, especially after her boyfriend, we'll call him Jesse, moved in with them. I knew he was bad for her. She was so vulnerable after Morgan's father decided not to be a part of their lives. She thought she couldn't do any better, so she clung to him. My feelings about this is that this was a very crucial time in her life and this is when she needed a positive person in her life that would encourage her and bring her self esteem back to life. This is not what she got.

When I would go home for visits Gary would try hard to spend time with me. He knew the pain I was going through and I am sure his guilt had a lot to do with this. But I new he was doing drugs. I could see it in his eyes. We would talk about it and I would try and assure him how much we loved him and I could see the pain in his eyes. I honestly though he was trying to get off whatever he was on. I was just not educated on the power of drugs and how it became the first and most important thing in their life and to what extreme people go to just to get their next high. Gary did try to take good care of Morgan and on days Rae could not get out of bed he would take care of her and cook for her. He absolutely could not stand the boyfriend and how he treated Rae. It was so obvious to everyone that came in contact with them, that he was bringing her down and down.

During this time I would receive mail, some signed, some anonymous and some was just paper clippings telling me of drugs in Beaver County. I received a letter telling me that I was "pathetic" leaving my mother to deal with my problems. What a horrible nightmare these years were and it would only get worse. I would go to the mailbox and try to open the mail so Whitey wouldn't see any of this mail. I knew it would upset him so much and besides I wasn't sure if he even knew what was going on. That was probably a big mistake on my part; I tried to hide all of this from him. Then I had the fear of him finding out. What a disaster. Going to the mailbox everyday became a nightmare. My hands would shake so bad and my heart would pound that I could feel it in my throat. Would there ever be piece in my family again?

Going to work became extremely difficult, I would be upset from the mail, I never knew what kind of a day Whitey would have and what if he needed me? Also I never knew what kind of a phone call I might get at work concerning the problems back in PA. To top things off, the office manager where I worked was not easy to get along with, to say it mildly. Not that I expected any type of special treatment, maybe just some understanding would have been nice. In spite of all the obstacles I had to continue working, we needed the money and I needed health benefits.

Well it was June 2003, I had been making my usual calls and talked to Rae this one weekend and when I asked her to talk to Gary she told me he had gone away for the weekend. I somewhat believed her but had my doubts that she was telling the truth. Every time I would call and no one would answer I would get sick with worry. Then I would call again and again until I talked to someone. Then the sick feeling in my stomach would go away. Calling them became an obsession with me.

On Monday I went to work as usual and got a call from Rae, Her words were " are you setting down? Gary is in jail". Oh my God, I new this would happen, why wouldn't he let us help him? Being at work I tried to stay calm but my friend

Julie could see that something was terribly wrong and came over to me. She would try to comfort, and support me. What would I have done without her? My next thoughts were of Gary and how is he, after all this is my son and he is in JAIL. My son in jail. This is horrible. How am I going to tell his father? I also know what Gary must have been going through and thinking about how this would affect us. This was not Gary, this was drugs.

My feelings; my heart hurts, I'm sick, angry and disappointed with the choices my children have made. I would pray, " Dear God, don't let me down, I need you to help my children." How would we survive without his help? How would I survive without my Gary?

June 6.....we have been on an emotional roller coaster, Gary's in jail, at least he's not doing drugs at the moment. We finally heard from him, I was so relieved to hear his voice. He was very emotional and asked that we please bear with him and support him during his detox. I could hear sorrow in his voice, I knew he didn't mean to hurt us, again it is the power of drugs. I would pray for God to watch over him and give me my son back.

Whitey had decided to drive home and take care of the legal aspect of the situation and see Gary.

We could not afford an attorney so he would have to deal with a public defender and that was that. Our hands were financially tied. Whitey went home, he drove home alone. With our financial situation as it was, someone needed to work and I guess that was me. It was not easy to stay behind. I had to put my trust in God to help Whitey have a safe trip home and give him the strength to be able to deal with the situation. Beside I thought that I had been trying to handle this on my own for several years, without him knowing. Now that he is aware maybe he will be able to do some good, I certainly was not able to help. I am so sorry for him. I am so confused. I don't know what to do, where to turn, who can help? I CAN DO NOTHING.

He made it home, oxygen and all. He was going to stay with Rae and Morgan so that he could see what was going on and make sure Morgan was okay. She was sure happy to see her pappy.

Gary had called again and was going through the program; his spirits seem to be good and is looking forward to a visit from his father. I'm not sure I could have handled that. Whitey managed to borrow enough money from a cousin to post bail and get Gary home. We tried not to rush the process as we thought it would be good for him to spend some time in jail. It was not easy to stay behind while all this was going on. I did have some support. Julie knew everything and was very supportive and non judgmental. That's what I needed at the time. Julie and I had such a bond that we knew we were brought together to help each other in our difficult times. We did and still do.

Whitey stayed there for a while, got Gary home and stayed to make sure that all seemed well. He felt that Gary was on the right track and was not doing any drugs while he was there. Now if he could only stay away from drugs and his friends, go to his scheduled hearing and pay his dues, maybe his life can get back on track.

It came time for Whitey to return home to Florida and I would make arrangements to go home to PA in a month or so. What else could I do? I asked myself over and over, should I have stayed in PA and left Whitey in Florida to deal with his illness alone? I know that many family members thought that's what I should have done. Maybe I should have moved in the house with them and watched over them like babies? I wonder if that would have worked? I don't know. I do know that I was trying very hard to do the right thing for everyone involved and I couldn't.

We kept in touch daily with Gary and Rae, I would not be able to sleep if I didn't talk to them each day. Many nights I would be unable to sleep so I would pray the rosary and as Aunt Rose would say, "on your knees." What a way to live. Our life is a mess. After several days of contact with Gary I was becoming a little comfortable in the fact that he seemed to be doing the right thing. As far as Rae and her boyfriend, I'll never feel comfortable about that. He's wrong for her.

July 3.....the dreaded day. I received a phone call from Rae, hysterical, saying " Mom, Gary OD." I guess there was no easy way to tell me so she just said it. There was silence on my end and noise and confusion on Rae's. "What do you mean"? "Is he okay" I screamed. I really don't remember the entire conversation. I do remember the day. At first the impact didn't hit me as to how serious this was, I thought he just passed out or had a reaction, I didn't realize the paramedics were there and he was almost dead. At that very moment they were trying to get him down the curved staircase and were having trouble making the bend and one of the spindles broke and they were able to get him down the stairs and into the ambulance. Rae told me my brother was there and I asked to speak to him, he furiously got on the phone and I said, "do I need to get right home?" He yelled, " you should have been home a long time ago". How stupid of me..."do I need to come right home"...I don't think I meant to say that...I was in shock. Those words will haunt me forever and so will his answer. I know he was extremely upset and he was stuck there with the task of telling mom.

I later had a dream and saw my father standing at the staircase sight. When I told Rae about the dream, she said that was the spot the spindle was broke. Isn't that interesting?

They were taking my son to the emergency room because of an overdose and he is 1200 miles away. I was hysterical and not able to think straight. Whitey knew from my conversation on the phone what was going on, what a mess....my heart is racing even as I write this. I needed someone to help me think straight. I called several friends and got a hold of someone to come over and help me make arrangements to go home as soon as possible. We called the hospital first and I spoke to the doctor and Rae. I was told he was alive but they did not know if there would be any brain damage. Of course my brother was also with him. Well I knew he was alive and I would be there in the morning. This just added to the guilt of me not being there for Gary, Rae and Morgan . Again my family members are dealing with my problems... what a mess. What about Morgan, is she seeing all this? I couldn't wait to get there.

Whitey was shocked as he really thought after being home and spending that time when Gary got out of jail, that he would be okay..again the power of drugs. We did find out that he took a combination of heroin and Valium.

Of course it seemed as though morning would never get here and I would pace all night in disbelief of what has happened. I took a walk around 1:00am to a place that Morgan and I call "our special place". We would go there to pray and ask for God's help when she would come and visit. I felt that my prayers were not being answered and surely God would listen to little Morgan when we would ask God to help Uncle Gary and her Mom. Morgan is my reason for survival, she is my rock. This "special place" was a small shelter by a lake in the village where we lived. As I reached the shelter I was praying, crying and begging for strength to face what was ahead. Please give me a sign that everything would be okay and I would see my son alive. Just then a very short rain came over the shelter as I could hear the drops hit the metal roof. I know this type of rain happens in Florida all the time, but that was good enough for me to call a "sign." I walked back to our condo and sat and waited until it was time to go to the airport.

I was picked up at the airport by Rae and taken directly to the hospital. Even going to the hospital was difficult, it was the hospital that I had worked in for 23 years and I knew a lot of people there. It was both emotional and embarrassing for me to go to that hospital.....I could not bear the fact that everyone would know that my son overdosed on drugs. I guess that is because I had not yet come to realize the fact that my son is a drug addict. There were so many people that I did not want to run into, I wanted to hide but I could not wait to be there by Gary's side. I knew he needed me more that ever and I wanted to assure him of our support. I would not go in the main entrance, to avoid seeing all the people from my old department. I went in the side entrance; it was closest to the ICU anyway. Okay, am I ready to see Gary? I was alone and didn't know what to expect. That's okay, that's the way I wanted it. Well when I entered the room he was hooked up to IV's, oxygen and he was sleeping. He was not on life support, which was good. As I approached him I called his name and held his hand. "It's Mom, I'm here Gary, and it's okay." He opened his teary eyes, but I'm not sure he could see me. He said over and over "it's the devil, Mom, it's the devil". I will never forget those scary words. I knew he was talking about the drugs. I could not believe this was happening. Was this a nightmare? I just kept thinking what has he done to himself. My Gary, my son. God please help us!

The doctors and I new he was not able to see clearly. They were not sure if that would be permanent of not. It would be a matter of time to see if his sight would come back completely. By this time I felt sure he was going to make it through, just not sure if he would be able to see again.

During the following days he improved a little every day. It was good to see him sit up in the chair and trying to eat. He would have difficulty reaching for objects on his tray and picking up the silverware was a task. He would miss the object and pick up silverware backwards and upside down because of his sight problem. Thank God he still had his sense of humor because we would laugh over some of these things.

In the meantime Whitey could not stay in Florida, so he decided to drive back to PA, again by himself. He did it straight through. He just wanted to get there to see Gary. I remember expecting him to arrive around 2:00 p.m. on the second day of his trip and he arrive early in the morning on that day. I couldn't believe my eyes as he entered my mom's house. He had driven straight through only stopping for little breaks and taking a nap in car. I don't know how he did it, but he did.

Soon Gary was moved out of ICU to a regular floor, other than his vision he was doing well, so he would soon be released. We weren't sure what to do when he was discharged. We did not want him to go back to the house and the old environment. Whitey and I were staying with my mother so we would bring him there and then back to Florida with us. The decision was made and he agreed. By this time it was the middle of July and we decided that I would fly back to Florida and return to work, as I left without any notice and if I didn't return soon they were going to have to replace me. It was best that I went back to work.

Gary and Whitey would stay until the end of July, as Gary wanted to stay for the family reunion, they drove back together. Gary would have to return in several months for a court date and serve whatever sentence he was given. Before I left we took Gary for a return visit with the doctors. They were amazed to see him and commented that he was very luck to be alive. He also went to be evaluated by our cousin, who has a therapy company, we were hoping to find out why he was having difficulty walking and reading.

We found out that his walking problem was because his peripheral vision was impaired. He could only see directly in front of him. He also could not control his shaking hands and we were not sure if this was permanent, only time would tell. We are sure his life was spared for some very special reason. He is very lucky and we are very fortunate to have him and I thank God for this miracle.

Gary and Whitey left the week after the reunion and had a safe trip to Florida we would spend the next several months just letting Gary to recuperate. Whitey would take him to the pool to soak up the sun. I was able to go to work. A job that I truly enjoyed would begin to turn sour, as the office manager was not real happy with me. Things at work were changing since I had returned from my son's life and death ordeal. I will not go into details about this because it is immaterial; it was just never the same again. I came close to leaving on several occasions. I still needed to work, Rae was not working and Morgan still needed a roof over her head, besides I needed the health insurance.

Gary was no trouble and it was good to have him with us. We would try and take him out occasionally. I remember the first time we went out eat. I had invited Julie to join us and meet

Gary for the first time. I thought he would enjoy some younger company and he did. Julie was a good friend and I remember her reading the menu to him because his vision was still impaired. We would continue to do some fun things on the weekends to keep him busy.

Soon he would have to return home for his court appearance. This was hard for all of us, we didn't want him to go, but he had to face whatever was ahead. We knew there would be more jail time and probation, but we anxious to put this ordeal behind and move forward. We had decided he would fly home alone. His sight was improving slowly but he assured us he would be able to do this. My concern was that he would not be able to read the signs at the airport but he did fine and my brother picked him up, took him to my mother's to stay. I would have felt better had I been able to go with him, but it was not to be. I continued to suffer from guilt over all this. My brother, doing what I should have been there to do, my mother giving Gary a place to live while he was there. It's easy for others to say your job shouldn't matter, but it does to a certain extent. I was still responsible for paying the house bills in PA and all those plane trips back and forth for the past several years. We made the best decisions we could at the time.

He went to his court hearing and received his sentence that was to begin in a couple months. He received permission to return to Florida to recuperate until the time he was to return to jail. That's exactly what he did. He spent 6 months in jail and was sentenced to 1-year house arrest. The house arrest he spent at my mother's and went to work for my brother during this time. I thank God he obeyed the rules, as he could have made things very difficult for Mom. We were concerned that some of his old friends would try and contact him and show up at Mom's, this could have been and disaster. However it didn't happen and Mom became very comfortable with him there. It was company for her and besides his days were spent working for my brother. This was good for him; he bonded with Aunts and Uncles every morning, as Mom's house is the meeting place for coffee in the mornings. They sit around the table and discuss all the town events and family situations. Sometimes you can't hear yourself think it gets so loud. He went to work, paid his fines and went to meetings when necessary and he received great support from the family. They always managed to get him where he needed to go, rain, sleet or snow. Again I felt guilty that could not be there to do this but they know how much it was appreciated. Whitey's health was not getting any better, however I did fly to PA when I could to see Mom, Gary, Rae and Morgan.

4
Rae's Addiction

During this time Rae was not doing well at all, her depression would make it almost impossible to get out of bed. She was miserable; she did things I would have never believed my daughter would do. She would do anything the "boyfriend" wanted her to do. She no longer could see right from wrong or just tried to block it out. Writing about this is more difficult than writing about Gary. This is my daughter, my friend, the mother of my beautiful Morgan. She was so blessed to have a daughter like she had, why couldn't she see that? This guy had a terrible hold on her and she let it happen. What happened to that strong girl I used to know? She was gone and I couldn't get here back.

She managed to take care of Morgan and that was about it. She hated herself more everyday and would take more and more pills not to face herself. She knew the pain she was causing her grandmother, her father and myself. Not to speak of the money this was costing us. She could not stay there with him any longer, she needed to come to be with us. I begged and begged. I threatened to take Morgan, she would threaten suicide. As Morgan was her reason for living.

I told her that I was going to sell the house and she would have to come and live here. She said she would go and live at the "boyfriends" grandfather's. It became apparent that she was not going to leave him and there was no way I would let her take Morgan to the grandfather's. I would just pray and ask for God help again and again. Many sleepless nights I would wake up and say my rosary.

November 2004....It was Thanksgiving Day, Gary was serving his sentence, and so Whitey and I were here in Florida alone. I was cooking to send food to Julie, as her mother was in the hospital dieing of lung cancer. I knew it would be their last Thanksgiving together and I was just trying to do something for her. She was always here for me. In the meantime I had made reservations for Rae and Morgan to come the beginning of December to spend Christmas. What Rae didn't know was that there would be no return ticket for them. That was the only way I could get them here and I had to do it. Too much time had passed and the situation was out of control. It didn't matter how angry she would be with me. Morgan would be here and she would get over it.

I took the food to Julie and I told her of my plan and said that if he would leave Rae it would make it easier because she would never leave him. Within the next day or so, Rae called and asked if we could get her ticket moved to an earlier date. They had some sort of blow up and she wanted out of there. I couldn't get her here fast enough. In a few days they arrived with one suitcase for each of them. They left everything behind. We were happy to have them finally. Maybe now we can get her life back on track and get the help she needed. We got Morgan into school and Rae soon got a job. They were doing so much better and so were we.

We were very crowded in our apartment and being a 55 and over community they were only aloud to be here temporarily. They got an apartment a few minutes away and it seemed to be fine. Summer came and I went part time at work, because Whitey's health was getting worse and he could not help with Morgan while Rae was working. So be it, that's what I did.

Rae had meet some friends at work that I had reservations about, but she had been doing so well I didn't say too much. After all we don't have to like everyone our children like. Rae got thrown a curve when the doctor she was working for sold his practice and the new owner hired all new employees; she was devastated and began to sink into depression again. I asked myself time and time again why is this happening to her, just when she seemed to be getting her life back together.

Finally, Gary's time was up and now we would get his probation transferred to Florida. It all happened, not quickly, but it did happen.

5
The Bankrupcy

Well it was bound to happen. After much discussion and careful though there was no way around this. We had become so much in debt caused by health problems and traveling back and forth this was the only way out. We hired an attorney, which in itself if not easy, You're filing bankruptcy because you don't have any money but you need money to file. It took us some time to pay the $2000 required by the attorney. We were able to keep our condo in Florida and our car. We lost the home in PA, which meant we lost the $23,000 we used for the down payment. Oh well that house was a nightmare anyway and I was glad to see it go.

I had to go home several times during the proceedings to clear out the house. Once while Gary was still there, so he was able to help me. Most of the time I would go there alone. I have asked so much of my family I refused to ask for any more help. At least I had my mother and her comfortable home to stay with. Whitey was not able to help at all.

6
Whitey's Lung Transplant

During all the events of the past several years, What about Whitey? He was not well at all. It has been impossible for me to give him the attention that he deserved. From his point of view he would just feel bad for me because I had to do so much alone. We understood each other and knew we would continue to do what we had to. I would feel bad for him and he would feel bad for me. We were used to surviving with problems.

Early summer of 2004 Whitey received a letter from a friend (Art) telling his of a procedure he had heard about that may benefit him. The procedure was called "Lung Volume Reduction Surgery." Art would follow up by sending information and the names of several hospitals where this procedure could be done.

I called the phone numbers and left messages for the transplant centers to return my call. Within a day I had received a call from the The Transplant Center at the Mayo Clinic in Jacksonville, Florida. I told them the situation and we would be in touch.

After Whitey had a short stay in a local hospital, I called The Mayo Clinic and made an appointment in August 2004. Testing began immediately to see if he would be a candidate for this procedure. We were told he would not, but had we ever considered a lung transplant? We had not, as it had never been suggested to us. None of the doctors who had treated him, either here in Florida and Pennsylvania had suggested it to us. Whitey immediately, without a second thought, wanted to go through with the extensive testing involved.

Testing begins and continues for months, making may four-hour trips to the Mayo Clinic and St. Luke's Hospital. Sometimes I would go with him, and sometimes Gary would go with him. Sometimes he had to make the trip alone.

During these months, there would be setbacks and he would be in and out of our local hospital. He was once told, as he went for a check-up with his primary doctor, that he was a time bomb. His oxygen level was low, blood pressure was high and heart rate too rapid. There was just too much pressure on his heart from his breathing.

He was admitted to St. Luke's in September for Cardio Version to regulate his heart rate, which was a success and he began to feel better. He continued testing and was told in November that he would be put on the transplant list. However, after being told the price of the anti-rejection medication and that insurance would not cover all of it, we had to try and find a way to pay for this medication. It could cost as much as $4000 per month. Well there was no way we could pay for this.

We were told to apply for Medicaid, which we felt sure would be denied. We applied anyway at the beginning o December. Whitey was told he should hear from them in 7-10 days. Time passed and we heard nothing. His health was declining rapidly. We made calls to the Medicaid office to try and find out the status of his case, with no luck, as no one had the answers. We got a lot of "that's not my department", "you need to talk too..." or "I'll transfer you." Before I could finish a sentence, they would transfer me again to the wrong person. One day after making about twelve calls, I ended up being transferred back to the person I started with. This was ridiculous and I was frustrated. It was useless. I guess we would just have to be patient. Even a letter to Jeb Bush was answerer by sending us an application for Medicaid.

The first week in January, my daughter called Medicaid again to try and find out what was going on. She went through the same thing I did. At this point, Whitey rarely left the bedroom and his breathing became increasingly worse. He could not even make it to his doctor's appointment on January 3rd, as he was too weak. He rescheduled the appointment for the 6th an I made it a point to go with him. We made it an it's a good thing, as his oxygen level was in the low 70's and the doctor admitted him to our local hospital.

Now the miracle begins.......When I came home from admitting him to the hospital, I called Elaine, the Social Worker at Mayo Clinic to see if there was something she could do. I asked her if she would please call Medicaid, maybe she would get an answer, or rush tings a little. I was afraid it we didn't get on that transplant list soon he would not make it. Elaine agreed to call but warned me that she usually she couldn't much more headway that we could. Five minutes passed and she called me back. Whitey had been approved Medicaid Share of Cost. I had never heard of this plan, but she said it would get him on the transplant. She then e-mailed the transplant team and go from there. Now all we would have to do is wait for and organ donor.

January 7th..while still in the local hospital, he doing a little better and they were able to bring his oxygen level up in the 90's.

January 8th, 12:30am my phone rings and it was Dr Keller from the Mayo Clinic, asking to speak to Mr. Harris as he has a possible lung. Now mind you this is only hours since he was put on the list. My reaction was in total shock, What?..We didn't even know the paper work went through. I was afraid to tell Dr. Keller that he was in the hospital, but I had no choice. He asked me some questions concerning Whitey's health and I suggested he talk to the admitting doctor, I was afraid I would say the wrong thing and he would not be able to get the transplant because of his severe condition. I would have to get Dr Reinberg's number because I was fumbling around and of course unable to find it.

I looked it up in the phone book and called the number. Remember it's 12:45am and I'm calling his office expecting to get and emergency number to call. In my amazement the doctor answered. Now you can never get a doctor on the phone and he answers at this hour at the office!! The two doctor spoke to one another and made some plans.

I called the children and told them to "pack their bags, they have a lung for Dad." All of our reactions were the same. "What?...We didn't know he was on the list yet." I told them I would call as soon as I knew more. An hour passed before I received a call from the doctor telling me that transportation plans were being made. I packed a bag and got ready to leave.

I arrived at the hospital around 3:00am. Whitey was wide-awake and anxious. His nurse was great taking care of all the transportation. I thought I would pick him up and drive him to Jacksonville myself. They said that was not possible. It would take some time to get a transport team to accompany him in the ambulance. When she gave me the information needed to take him, there was a slight hurdle. The ambulance company needed payment of $2000 to take him. There was no way we could come up with the money and we had no credit cards do to the bankruptcy. What were we going to do? The nurse got the ambulance company on the phone for me to talk to. I asked why they couldn't bill his insurance and send us a bill for the remainder, truthfully I don't remember the answer. All I knew is I needed $2000. They knew his condition and I begged and told them he would die if we didn't get him there. I would just have to take him against medical advice, anything not to miss the opportunity to receive this lung. I went into Whitey's room to let him know what was going on with the ambulance. His eyes filled with tears and disappointment. At that very moment, the nurse came into the room and told us the ambulance agreed to bill our insurance and send us the remaining bill. Great news, we would be on our way soon, around 6:00am I just kept thinking we would be to late for the lung. We were soon on are way, it was around 7:00am by the time I picked up the family and the ambulance would arrive to transport Whitey. We all arrived at St. Lukes around 11:00am. Whitey was taken to a room and tests began to be sure this would not be a "dry run". This was the first time I had heard about a "dry run" that even after you have been called in for surgery, there is a possibility that it could be a dry run. This could happen for many reasons. In our case it was a go. We began calling relatives and friends to tell them of the good news and ask for prayers. My cousin Greg and Sally from Jacksonville arrived at the hospital to give us moral support and stayed with us until surgery was complete. Still this was happening so fast, could this be true, we are getting a new lung, a new chance at life. We were still in disbelief that this was really happening.

Surgery was not as long as we had anticipated and we were soon called and informed that everything went well and we would be able to see him soon. It was probably and hour after surgery when we went into ICU to see him. He was doing very well and resting comfortably. It was a long day for all of us, as no one slept the previous night so we went to our hotel to get a good nights rest.

The next morning to our amazement when we went into ICU, Whitey was setting up and the nurses were massaging him, he was already off all oxygen and his color was great even the color of his fingernails was pink. Something we hadn't seen in a very long time. He was moving around as if he had some minor surgery, he amazed us all and we were so proud of him.

Now we needed to decide who would stay with him to be his caregiver. It was supposed to be me but since this all happened so quickly and I hadn't turned in my notice at work and Rae Lynn was not currently working, it was decided that she would stay for a while and then I would relieve her sometime soon.

As it turned out I was not comfortable with Rae staying in Jacksonville, something was just not right, she was doing what she had to do, but she seemed so depressed and I had my suspicions that she was taking to much medication. I could tell in her voice and she was very defensive about everything I questioned her on. Could this be? Another hurdle to conquer.

I was being pressured at work to give then a date as to when I was leaving, so I turned in my notice for Febuary. Rae and I would trade places. At this time I knew for sure that Rae had s substance abuse problem. As I stayed in Jacksonville I worried constantly about Rae. Here we go again!!

Whitey was recuperating extremely well and required very little help from me. He was able to keep track of his medication and when to take it, this was not an easy task. He would spend about 45 minutes 3 times a day on medication, blood pressure and temperature monitoring. Every day he would go for physical therapy at the transplant center. He was really in the swing of things and he felt so good, it was a blessing. The friends we made at the transplant center, both patients and employees were also a special blessing. They were great for each other and the caregivers were also very involved in the recovery process. We met a lot a very special people through the heart/lung support group. We couldn't have made it without their support and the continuous support of the staff at St Luke's.

While staying in Jacksonville we tried to stay in close touch with the family. I talked to Gary, Rae and Morgan every day sometimes twice a day. I was confident that Gary was on track but I was very concerned about Rae and Morgan. It turned out I had good reason Rae was taking a lot of pain medication and she was going down hill fast. Again I was put in a situation where I needed to be in two places and that was not possible. We usually saw each other on the weekends and I was sure Rae was taking pills. I would confront her continuously she would just deny it and we would fight.

We came home for Easter and stayed over one night. Whitey was really anxious to be in his own home after being in a hotel since January 8th. Morgan and I went to church Easter Sunday. I was very emotional that day and I couldn't get Rae out of my mind. Morgan and I went into the candle room at the church and I wrote a note on a piece of paper and placed it in the hands of Jesus. It was a request that I was asking for help again with Rae and I was putting her in his hands. I knew she was headed for big trouble. Something was going to happen, I could just feel it. Well we returned to Jacksonville for Whitey to continue his therapy and recovery process, his 3 months would be over soon and hopefully he will be able to return home. Two days passed and I received a call from Rae telling me she was in trouble and I needed to come home to pick Morgan up at school. She was going to rehab to get help for her problem. Isn't this just grand?? I can't even tell you what all went through my mind, anger, disappointment, frustration and relief. It was 11am and we would be able to make it home by 4 to pick Morgan up. It was very difficult to even tell Whitey what was going on but I had no choice, we were in the car going for a little drive when I received the call. I suggested that I just drive home myself, take care of what needed done, and then return to Jacksonville. He took the news as well as could be expected. However he insisted he drive me home and then drive back to Jacksonville that evening. So that is what we did. I couldn't believe Rae put herself and her family in this position. But on the other hand I was hopeful that she would now get the help she needed. She actually sounded relieved on the phone. I knew she needed a lot of therapy to pull her out of the darkness she has been living in for the past five years.

I managed to get home in time to pick Morgan up at school. She was quite surprised to see me and I worried about what to tell her. I simply told her that her mom was entering a rehab center to get off the pills she was taking. Morgan understood and she had spent so much time with me that she seemed very comfortable, that would make things easier. I assured her we would all be fine and that her mom would be getting the help she needed. That was in March, 2005. Whitey went back to Jacksonville to finish his recovery without me. Thank God he was able to drive. What a strong man he was. He amazed even me, who knew him better than anyone. Since his surgery and with a second chance at life he was so calm and understanding. He assured me he would be okay and I had to stay home and take care of Morgan. I stayed home to deal with the situation there and he continued his stay in Jacksonville. Morgan, Gary and I would go on the weekends to Jacksonville for visits until he was discharged. During this time it would always be a struggle to get his medication and make sure we kept everything straight so that we could submit the proper bills to Medicaid so that we would meet our share of cost. There was no way we would have been able to pay for the thousands of dollars worth of medication he was taking. There was an article printed on line from the Mayo Clinic about our situation. It is as follows:

Mayo Clinic Story of Gary Harris: The Story About Medical Miracle Financial Tragedy

Medical triumph, financial tragedy

Gary Harris and his wife Patty were stuck. Gary's health was deteriorating rapidly. To survive, Gary needed a lung transplant. Although Gary and Patty both worked full time and had health insurance and disability, they were still financially strapped trying to cover medical bills.

The Harris family, including two adult children and a grandchild, sold their three bedroom home in Beaver Falls, Pa., and moved to a one-bedroom condominium in Florida. They were closer to Gary's doctors at Mayo Clinic in Jacksonville, but still desperate for a way to pay for Gary's lung transplant and the lifelong medications.

"We knew we wouldn't get a transplant for Gary if we didn't have the means to pay for his anti-rejection drugs, as much as $4,000 per month," says Patty. "We thought we would lose him."

After many phone calls, Patty was able to secure financial assistance from Share of Cost Medicaid and Gary was approved for his lung transplant.

In January 2005, Gary had a successful transplant, but he's no longer able to work. Patty was forced to retire early to take care of her husband. She lost her health insurance and does not have the means to pay for private health insurance. To make matters worse, the Harris's no longer have AARP coverage due to cost of living in Florida. Although a portion of Gary's medication costs is covered by Share of Cost Medicaid, the remaining fees are still overwhelming.

"It takes every cent we have just to live -- we don't have any extra money to pay for Gary's prescriptions or additional health insurance" says Patty.

The Harris's have declared bankruptcy. "Our story is a medical triumph but a financial tragedy" she says.

What about Rae? Well she entered a rehabilitation program, which would last for 18 months. There was no choice about how we would handle this. We gave her our support to get through the very rigorous military based program ahead. Morgan was very comfortable with us so that transition did not seem to be difficult. We explained to Morgan that her mom was in rehab so that she could stop taking all the pills. She seemed glad and understood. Gary was now working, but would not have his drivers license for several months, but that's was okay he was making progress. Whitey was strong enough and feeling really good so he would take Gary back and forth to work. Besides that gave Whitey purpose and he felt good about being able to do something to help out. We were able to visit Rae twice a week and we did. Morgan was not allowed to see her until she moved to the next level. So the phones calls would make her happy.

Rae seemed to be stronger every day and she seemed to thrive on the severe discipline in this program. During our visits we have good talks and she wrote some of the most beautiful letters I have ever read. Some of which I will share:

As much as we gave our support, we also let her know how very disappointed we were. She also knew she failed us when we needed her the most. Not only did she hurt her family, she gave us added stress and worry to deal with at a most difficult time. I was very angry and disappointed. Each week at our visits I could see dramatic changes in her face, the twinkle was coming back into her eyes and peace was coming over her face. This would bring us comfort and hope. She needed to be well to be able to raise her daughter. Her health was not that great, her blood pressure was out of control, her thyroid was out of whack and her stomach would bother her continuously. I'm sure her weight gain did not help and the pills she had taken made a mess out of her digestive system.

This would soon all be under control and she was put on a cardiac diet the proper thyroid medication. Soon she began to take of the weight and she continued to look brighter and better at every visit. There would be some problems during this time but she handled them. This was a very difficult program and I wasn't sure she would be able to complete it. The counselors were there for her and she could tell them things she could never tell her family. She was able to express a lot of her inner feelings and get over the hurts she had experienced with Morgan's father and "the boyfriend" that had treated her so badly. Plus I am sure there is a lot of feelings she expressed that I don't know and I don't know that I really want or need to know.

Gary is in recovery

Rae is in recovery

Whitey is in recovery from surgery.

During Rae's recovery program she would write the most amazing letters to all of us. I have kept them all and she became a true inspiration to me. I would like to share some of them with you:

4/1/05

"Dad, I'm sorry I've disappointed you so much. I am not a bad person, I still have a good heart. I wish I could go back and change the last five years. How much I have learned. I've hurt so many people. I hope to be forgiven someday. I want to be a strong person again. I want to be a great mom, maybe as great a parent as you and mom have been to me. I hope you can forgive me and have faith that I can get better and we can all be happy again."

5/7/05

'"I really am blessed to have a supportive family, a lot of the girls in here don't have that. They are on their own and have nothing. I took everything for granted, even my life. I can't believe it took this for me to step back and look at all of that. Sometimes I don't like to think about that, because I don't like the person I was, I'm not sure who that was but it wasn't me. I'm coming back healthy and strong, mind body and soul.

5/16/05

"I pray for God to help me keep an open mind, my heart filled with love and keep myself and my family healthy safe and strong. I pray for everyone after that. I talk to Pap, and then I say hi to everyone in heaven like Gramma Esoldo, Uncle Al, Uncle Bill, Uncle Red, Aunt Leah and Gram Harris. And anyone else I can think of at the time. This helps me sleep."

Rae did a lot of soul searching and read from many different books here are some of the inspiration saying she has sent to me.

"Remember: The future belongs to those who believe in the beauty of their dreams."

"We all have a great future because I know my dreams and dreams do come true, and it's okay to dream big."

These are little reading she sent me from the book "A Time for Joy"..I love all of these.....

"To accept ourselves as we are means to value our imperfections as much as our perfections --I will value myself today both for my perfections and especially for my imperfections."

"Choosing positive thoughts and making positive choices fill me with new strength, confidence and excitement. I can feel positive energy flow through me with every positive thought I choose."

"Today I am hanging in no matter what, even when my conscious mind want to give up. I will reach for that healthy, loving part deep within me and with the help of prayer and meditation and the good people in my life. I will find a rainbow."

"Today I know that I am not the best or the worst, I am just me."

"Recovery is a path...not a sudden landing. I know that one step at a time I am making progress today.

What wonderful sayings....

We would continue getting many letters from Rae, some were wonderful and some would be sad, but we knew she was growing with each day and we could see her coming back to us. As she said, "body, mind and soul.

Whitey would have some good days and some bad days, but as long as he was home and not in Jacksonville he would be Gary's taxi service and seemed to be glad to help. This also gave Gary and Whitey some time together. Rae finally moved to the other side of the program, which was a step up and after she completed all the levels she would graduate from the program. As busy as we were the time seemed to fly by. We could finally take Morgan to visit and she never missed one, even though it was early on Saturday mornings. We had to set through a 45 minute educational lecture to help understand the program and what the residents are going through. Morgan did well, as this was difficult for adults to set through let alone small children. It was all worth it when she could see her Mom's smiling face. Rae would dwindle away 80 pounds during these months and began looking and feeling like she did years ago. We would all feel better just looking at her. Whitey was so proud of her as was I.

Whitey had a lot of sets backs, a lot of it was due to anti rejection medication, which would take care of one problem but cause another. He went through a spell, where he was drinking alcohol and hiding it from us. We knew what he was doing as his demeanor would change with one drink. He didn't drink a lot but with the medication he was taking it didn't take much to affect him. Gary and I would become very upset when we thought he was drinking and we both confronted him. I felt badly and sorry for him. Maybe I should have let it go, after all he's been through a lot and if he wants to drink so be it. Easier said that done, I could see him taking such good care of himself, taking all his medication and keeping all his appointment and then occasionally drinking alcohol. His medication would sometimes make him dizzy and cause him to fall. He did not need to add alcohol to his system. Although the drinking seemed to stop he continued to become dizzy and fall quite often. When this would happen he would feel so bad thinking this was a problem for me and he didn't want that. As I said earlier all we ever did was worry about each other.

In March, Gary was able to get his drivers license and he could drive himself to work. This was good. He took Whitey's car and we would use Rae's car. March and April 2006, Whitey felt so good he said he wanted to start to golf. He said, " I feel so good, I'm scared." I just said "well don't be scared, just enjoy feeling good." I may have said that to him, but I also was scared I didn't think he looked real good. His color was good but he looked very puffy and swollen in his face and neck. We kept blaming it on the medication, as his feet didn't seem to be swollen so we didn't think it was water retention.

It was actually around May 1st he said he needed to call the Mayo Clinic, but Morgan was making her First Communion of May 7th, and he knew if he called they would put him in the hospital. He chose to wait. Morgan's Communion was beautiful and Whitey made it to church and pick up the cake and then on to join everyone at the lunch for Morgan's celebration. He was very tired and looked very puffy, everyone was very concerned.

Monday morning when I returned from taking Morgan to school he was packed and trying to get in touch with someone at the transplant center. He did, and was told to come directly to the center. I wanted to drive him but he insisted he could do it himself. I convinced him to take the cell phone, which he hated, but he did. It's a good thing because that day was a day of fires all along I 95 and he experienced many detours, I was so worried it took him 6 or 7 hours to make a 4 hour trip. We called each other until he reached the hospital. He remained calm through the traffic and said as long as he wasn't moving around he was fine, again, I felt very concerned, guilty and so worried. He was stubborn and wanted me to stay at home for Morgan.

He was admitted immediately upon his arrival. We were all relieved because we knew they would be able to fix whatever was going on with his body. His doctors were the best and Whitey would go along with whatever they would decide to do for him. He kept a very positive attitude, I don't know how he did it. He told the doctors to do everything they could until there was no more to do. We talked at least twice a day for the next week, they trying to eliminate the fluid build which led to concern for his kidneys. I had made arrangements to go to Jacksonville for Mother's day weekend to spend time with him. He was told he would have to stay there even when he was discharged for a series of treatments that had to be done there for insurance purposes. Gary and some of my friends would take care of Morgan so I would be able to stay several days, especially if he would be discharged I would be able to be with him and get him settled in a hotel room.

The social worker had encouraged us earlier to apply for Charity Care that would help us with lodging when we were in Jacksonville. They made reservations for me at the place we usually stayed and I left after I took Morgan to school. He didn't get to leave the hospital while I was there, he was just not eliminating enough fluid, even with the chest tube. Again, he said he felt pretty good. I wonder what really was going on in his mind. I don't think he ever let me know his true feeling about himself. I was always afraid to ask, because I didn't want him to think I thought it was bad and I never mentioned that I didn't think he was going to make it. He never let me know if he thought that also. Were we really hiding from ourselves. Protecting one another from the pain of what may come.

I know he was disappointed that he was not able to leave the hospital. I stayed until Monday, we decided Morgan and I would come back to Jacksonville as school would be over for the year.

Then as if that wasn't enough he began bleeding everytime he would bump his arms the slightest. From all the medication the skin on his arms became like cellophane paper and he would bleed from his skin. This had been an ongoing problem at home but a bandaid would take care of the problem. Now it was almost out of control. What must have been going through his mind.

He was finally discharged from St Luke's to the hotel where he would stay to continue treatment. Morgan and I would join him in a week as school would be over for the summer. He was discharged with oxygen on a temporary bases. He didn't seem upset over all this he just took one day at a time and looked forward to Morgan and I going to Jacksonville. I, like Whitey, felt very confident in whatever his doctors were doing for him, we knew if anyone could make him feel well they could. We never talked about the possibility that maybe he would never come home again. He had the most positive attitude of any person I have met. If he had negative thoughts he didn't express them any of us.

As he was staying at the hotel we began making plans for Morgan and I to join him. We didn't want to take my car there because then we would have two there and Gary would not have a way to work. He insisted that he could drive half way and Gary would drive us the other half and we would meet. So that's what we could do over the weekend. We were all anxious to get together and I was very anxious to be with him and stay until this problem was resolved..

Friday morning I received a call from Whitey, he was in the Emergency room at St. Luke's. He had a spell at the hotel, it was his breathing, so he call

911 and the ambulance arrived to transport him to the hospital. How horrible this must have been for him, there alone and I'm sure very frightened. He cried on the phone because he had to tell that he was in the ER. Then he assured me that he was doing better already and they would admit him. I told him I would be there as quickly as I could although we would have to get Gary home from work to drive us there. However, as it turned out, our very good friends, Mary and Larry we leaving that evening to begin their journey back to New Hampshire and we would ride to Jacksonville with them. It's funny the way things work out. Mary and Larry had a situation the previous week were as Larry was in the hospital dealing with an illness of his own, they were supposed to leave the weekend before and their trip was postponed by one week. It is so true that God puts you where you're supposed to be at any given time. That week delay made it possible for us to arrive a little sooner and our dear friends went into the hotel with me. I didn't know what I would see when I would open the door. As we went in the room I immediately realized that he was much worse than he let on. There was oxygen tanks lying all over the place and the bed sheets had blood everywhere. That may not sound to bad, but Whitey was very neat and I knew by the looks of the room that he was having a difficult

time. I wanted Mary and Larry to come into the hospital to see Whitey as I knew he would want to see them. Whitey was very concerned about Larry a week ago when they thought Larry had a heart attack. I knew that they had to see each other, I felt sure that with both of them being very ill that one of them might not be there on their return to Florida in the fall. When we arrived to Whitey's hospital room he was so glad to see us and aside from the fact that his arms were a mess and bleeding so bad, he looked pretty good. He was laughing and making jokes as usual. What a guy!! Here I was concerned about him losing all this blood and worried about when are they going to clean this up and on and on. He just took it in its stride and said they had just replaced the bandages and bed linens and I should not worry. He also said that they were trying to regulate his medications to clot this bleeding. He never once gave me the idea that he was tired of all this or that he was ready to give. He just would say you got to do what you got to do.

The visit with our friends was short and sweet as they had a long drive ahead on their way home to New Hampshire. I got the keys to our car, which had been parked in the hotel parking lot. Mary and Larry drove us back to the hotel where we said our good byes for the summer. We had driven during the night so Morgan and I tried to get a little rest before returning to the hospital. We were to restless so we just went to the hospital and spent time with Whitey. We spent the day going in and out of his room. His spirits were very good and he was so comfortable with the staff, he was such a good patient. The more time I spent with him the more I admired him for his strength and sense of humor. However, I did realize that this was a little more than I had bargained for and I felt sure that Morgan did not need to be there. I thought that he would possibly be there for a few days and we would take him back to hotel and spend time with him there. It became apparent almost immediately that this was not going to be the case and I would have to make arrangements to get her home. Between Gary and my friend Louann they would take care of her. Louann would watch her during the day and Gary would pick her up after work. Louann offered to drive to Jacksonville to pick her up, but I decided that I would meet her half way on Sunday as long as things were stable with Whitey.

What about Morgan during these last several years? This child has seen way too much for her age. She was present when Gary had his accident. She lived with her mother during her terrible depressing years. She went to school one morning with her Mom and then she didn't see her again for many months. She watched her Pappy, who she loved like a father, become a very sick man. Morgan is my life and my strength. I will do whatever is in my power to keep her happy and healthy during this ordeal.

During the day on Saturday Whitey received a call from one of our good friends from Pennsylvania to see how he was doing. I put him on the phone and he told her "I'm doing good and I'll beat this." That statement gave me a good feeling and again I felt sure he would be fine and this was just another hurdle or "bump in the road" that transplant patients encounter. Morgan and I left the hospital early that evening to go back to the hotel, Whitey insisted he was okay and that I should meet Louann half way so she wouldn't have to drive all the way. I agreed as long as he was good in the morning. Sunday morning we arrived at the hospital to find him in good spirits and he said he would be fine and for me to go to meet Louann. He always let me believe that he didn't want me to sit there all day he just liked to see me pop in and out all day long and that what I did. Was it because he knew I had a hard time with sitting still? Morgan said her goodbye to her Pappy and laid her head on his arm to give him a hug. I watched him as we walked out of the room. It really bothered me, wondering if he was thinking that he might not see her again. After all Whitey was her father image and she was the love of his life. He felt so bad that she had gone through so much tragedy at her young age. We have both become very protective of her and I know she was one of his major concerns. We left to meet Louann and I was back at the hospital before dinner. When I arrived he was asleep but woke up when I came in the room. He seemed startled for a few seconds, and then he said, " I had the strangest thing happen to me, the room and everything in it is upside down". I said that I would call a nurse and he said, "No, it's turning around again." I stayed a while and we never mentioned it to anyone, he probably just had a dream from all the medication he was taking. Now when I think of that episode I truly feel he had an out of body experience and he was looking at himself from overhead. We never even mentioned that to anyone other than to our family.

I left to go back to the hotel early that evening. I felt pretty comfortable about leaving and felt sure he would be okay and I would see him in the morning. It was lonely at the hotel without Morgan, so I watched TV and worked on a puzzle trying to relax. Just then the phone rang, it was the hospital. I was told that Whitey went into respiratory distress and he was calling for me, I should come over immediately as they were going to intubate. I was there in 10 minutes. He was being wheeled out in his bed already intubated and heavily medicated, I don't think he knew I was there. His transplant doctor was right there at the head of his bed along with other staff members. Dr Keller looked at me and said," We're taking him to ICU, we have a lot of work to do." I was stunned and felt that I was going to pass out, this was such a shock to me. Was I that naive that I didn't see this coming? I immediately called my nearby cousins Greg and Sally, they were about 45 minutes from the hospital and I needed to talk to someone. They got in the car and came to the hospital to be with me. I told Gary not to come at this time until I knew more about his condition. We stayed until he was stabilized and we were able to see him. He was in a medically induced coma on a respirator at the time, we talked to him and assured him we were there, not sure if he even heard us. My understanding was that he would be kept heavily medicated until they would be able to take him off the breathing machine. I understood and stayed calm, I thought he would be off this machine in a day and he'll be fine. Monday and Tuesday passed, he was not ready. I knew his wish was not to be on any life support. However the doctors felt it was too soon to make that decision. The children and I talked it over and agreed to go along with whatever the doctor's thought was in his best interest. Every day I would ask the doctors when they thought he would be ready to come off the machine. It just was not happening and besides now they also put him on dialysis, this also was hopefully to be temporary. His kidneys were failing, things did not look good. Gary took off work , brought Morgan, and came to spend some time with us. Rae was not able to leave rehabilitation, our contact was through her counselor. His vitals were better over the weekend while Gary was there and we thought maybe he would be okay. His friends from the Heart Lung Transplant group came to give their support and visit Whitey continuously. Whitey and I talked about kidney dialysis the week before he went on this life support. He told me that if it was temporary that would be okay but he did not want to be on dialysis to live. They tried to wean him off some of his medicines so they could try and take the ventilator from him, he became restless and combative so that did not work.

In the meantime, I debated about telling his family how serious his condition was. We had been in touch and keeping them updated, but I still had thought he would rally and would be able to tell me whether or not to ask them to come and see him.

It was becoming more apparent every day that he was not coming back, so I called. His brother and sisters made the trip from Pennsylvania to Florida to see him and I thank God they did.

Then Monday June 12th came and when I went into his room they were rushing around and cleaning him up. I knew that this was not good, as all his organs were shutting down the dialysis and breathing machines were keeping him alive. It became apparent the time had come to make a decision. The doctors and I talked it over and said that they had tried everything possible as they had hoped he would come around, but nothing was working.

I talked to Gary and we were in agreement that this was exactly what Whitey did not want and he would say "no more". Well the time had come to make that dreaded decision. When I spoke to Gary, he agreed that this is exactly what dad did not want and with all that was going on at his beside it was time. Gary has suggested one thing and it was something that was on my mind also. He said "Mom you might want to wait until after June 14th". You see that is Rae's Birthday and we felt that it would not hurt to wait another couple of days. I agreed, however when I spoke to Rae and when I told her what was happening to her father, she said not to worry about her.

She knew from her medical background what was going on with him and his strong feelings about what he wanted and what he did not want. She agreed with her brother and myself, the time had come. Dialysis was not working and his kidneys had stopped his body was telling us what to do.

His family arrived from Pennsylvania and got to see him, but we are not sure if he knew they were there. His two sisters, Sue and Donna along with his brother Glenn and brother-in-law Jim talked to him and let him know they were there, he was not able to respond at all. But from what I understand some people believe they can hear you when they are in that state, we just kept talking. I told them of our plans to remove a life support on Tuesday the 13th and they were also in agreement. I thank God that they were with me and that they got to see him.

Needless to say Monday was a sleepless night, all the thoughts that went through my head as I waited for Tuesday morning to arrive. Deep down I knew he would die sometime on Tuesday and the thought that if I kept the machines on he would live longer. What gave me the right to decide this? No matter how much you have talked it over with your loved one and family it was still our decision. I went through all his papers to be sure I was reading everything correctly and took it to the hospital the next morning for the doctors to review. Everything was in order except on the living will he had my name as power of attorney and then Gary Jr. I'm sure he thought that's the way it was supposed to be, but my name should have been on both lines. All it meant was that the doctors would have to have a conference call with Gary to be sure we were in agreement.

In Gary's own words, that was the hardest decision he had ever had to make. The doctor's talked to everyone and we all felt confident that they were doing what he wanted. He always said "Doc do what you can until you can't do any more", and that's exactly what they did. After a couple of hours they had removed everything and we were all able to see him. I let his family go in first and then they insisted that I go in alone, I'm not sure I wanted to be alone, so the Social Worker offered to come with me if I wanted her to. Elaine had been our support for the past two years and I was very comfortable with her, I couldn't have made it without her. As I entered by his bedside, I just looked at him and I had no words to say. Elaine began asking me questions about our relationship and other incidents and it really got me talking and telling stories. I hope he enjoyed them. It did not take long, he only lasted a short time without the life support. By 12:22 p.m. he was gone, that's when I knew we had made the right decision. What can I say, it was horrible, but anyone that has gone through the process of losing someone has gone through the same thing. I just felt so bad for Whitey, he wanted to live every day that was given to him, he showed unbelievable strength and an attitude that I would never be able to duplicate if in his situation. Having my in-laws there with me was so perfect and it's exactly what he would have wanted. My children were not able to be there at that time, so what would I have done without them?

We stayed at the hospital for a while to make some type of arrangements. Elaine never left me until approximately 5:00 p.m. I had to get back to the hotel to pick up Morgan. A member of the Support Group had taken her for the day and I wanted to be with her. Whitey's family insisted on taking Morgan and I to dinner that evening so that we could be together and that's what we did. None of this seemsed real to me anyway.

I had been in touch with the clergy at the hospital and made arrangements for a mass in the chapel there for Thursday morning. Gary was coming up to be at the service and stay with me until we left to return to West Palm Beach. Rae was not able to leave her rehab but she had a lot of support by her piers and therapist. I knew she was better there. Her therapy had been so intense we did not want to jeopardize anything. Her father would have wanted it this way. We knew her heart was with us.

I made the arrangements for his cremation, with the help of "Walter", a dear friend and had his remains sent back to Beaver Falls, PA where there would be a funeral in the near future.

Thursday came and it was time to go to the service. It was so perfect and fitting for this man. He loved the Mayo Clinic and the people that worked there and they knew it. It showed by his continuous good attitude and sense of humor. They all spoke so highly of Gary "Whitey" Harris. We felt they had gone above and beyond for the family and we will never forget them. Doctors, staff and members of the Support Group attended the service, which meant so much to Gary and myself. After the service and refreshments sponsored by the Support Group we all parted and went our separate ways. My in-laws headed back to Pennsylvania and Gary and I decided to leave the next morning. I had mixed emotions about leaving Jacksonville, and I still do. That is the last place I saw my husband and that is where I said good by to him. Besides I too love the people and miss seeing them, after all they were a very special part of our lives for two years. I plan to go back and see everyone soon. I also have very mixed feelings about the passing of 2006. Most people feel that you should just hope for a better year ahead. To me, 2006 is gone right along with Whitey and his year is gone, not sure if that makes any sense to anyone but me. It just makes everything so final. Whitey truly is at peace and no longer has to struggle for each breath and that is what I have to think about.

When I arrived back in West Palm, that evening all my friends from around the area were there with food, friendship, support and a lot of "Whitey stories" and there were plenty. We laughed and cried together.

Now I have to get ready for the trip back to Pennsylvania and make all the arrangement for burial. Morgan and I will be the only ones going.

During the time I was waiting to go back to Beaver Falls, someone called to come and see our condo, which had been for sale for about a year, so by some miracle I sold it. It's so funny because Whitey wanted to sell it so bad, so that Morgan could have her own room. Our place was so small and for the past year Morgan and I had been sleeping on a air mattress in the living room and gave the bedroom to Whitey. He felt so badly about that, it didn't bother us too much, but it really bothered him, he promised Morgan she would get her room. Now that looks like a possibility. I accepted the offer made on the condo and now I would have to look for a place to rent. That's okay, this will keep me really busy and give me a lot to think about and a lot to do. In the time between now and leaving for Pa. I looks at several townhomes with my friend and realtor and we found several that I liked and where Morgan would not have to change schools. LouAnn would take care of all the paper work and let me know what townhouse we would get into. The rest would have to take place when I got back from Pa.

I made plane reservations and we were on our way.

My brother picked us up at the airport and took us to my Mom's. She was waiting for us to arrive, it was difficult for her to see me knowing that I lost my husband and she was not able to be with me. I was okay though, it didn't feel like I was home to bury my husband, just home for a visit. There were church arrangement and cemetery arrangement to make, so everything was tentative, as we had to be sure that Whitey's ashes had arrived at Grandview Cemetery. They arrived on Monday and services were held on Wednesday. It was a truly glorious day and he received all the respect he deserved. I greeted friends and relatives at the church where we had a mass of Christian burial for him. My family was very involved in the mass and helping with the arrangements. The eulogy was given by my cousin Michael. Michael and Whitey were very close especially in Michael younger football days, when Whitey took Michael to Joe Namath football camp in Connecticut. Michael's words were so appropriated for the occasion, I couldn't have said anything better or even as well. I was very happy with my choice of Michael.

The day was overwhelming for me and I know Whitey was pleased. Beside family, there were classmates of his and mine present. Longtime friends of both of ours. A special guest to arrive was his lifelong friend and classmate Joe Namath, who attended and participated in the mass service. I had hoped he would come, but with his very busy schedule I wasn't sure he would be able too. Our dear friends Flicka and Dino were at my side and also helped by carrying the ashes and transporting me from place to place. His dear friend Rocky from Tampa also make the trip to PA, which I will be forever grateful, Rocky was my escort as my brother took care of Mom.

After the Mass we all rode to the cemetery to say our final goodbye. It was a beautiful sunny day as we made the ride but as soon as we got to the site there was a slight down poor of rain, that no one was prepared for. That made for a short and sweet departure. It was almost like he got the last word and said "enough is enough". On that note we went to my Mom's for refreshments and just a lot of good talk about everything. The day lasted all evening as many of my friends that were unable to attend the service visited later. As I said it was a glorious day and I shall never forget it and all the family and friends that were there in his honor. As I would talk to many of his friends I would catch myself thinking, "I can't wait to tell Whitey who I saw today". My hope is that he knew what a beautiful service there was for him and how much he was cared about. I think he did, as that little down poor of rain was a sign.

I stayed for about a week, but had to return to West Palm Beach to begin packing and finding a place to move. With the help of good friends everything fell into place and we moved into a larger place and Morgan could finally have her own room. We made the move into our new place and began our lives without Whitey present in our daily lives. We felt him with us and still do, he is greatly missed and talked about often. We all feel better when we talk about him. There are times when all I see is him struggling to breath and laying their on that hospital bed, hooked up to all the machines that were keeping him alive. That is a sight I will never be able to forget.

Rae is getting a lot of support from rehab and is continuing to do very well as we continue our weekly visits until the time she can come home to be with us. Gary doesn't say too much, but I hope that if he feels the need to talk, he will. We now have to move on to make Whitey as proud of us as we are of him.

It would not be long until Rae would be released from rehab and be home with Morgan and myself. She would come home much stronger, spiritual and with a much greater appreciation of family. It's been a long 18 months not to have her with me and certainly at a time when I needed her the most, but for some reason it was meant to be this way and we all made it through. Gary continues to be a great source of help to Morgan, Rae and myself. He has now become the head of the family. It's funny how things happen and how all these tragic situations have brought us back to be the family that we used to be. Well almost, we are missing our father and husband. It is great to have my children back in my life and also for them to become responsible, sensitive, caring adults that had been lost somewhere, for some time. I think that the statement "we have been blessed" is so over stated but, I must say we have all been very blessed with this great gift of life after tragedy. Ten years ago if anyone had told me what the future had in store for my family, I think I might have curled up and crawled into a hole. It's better we don't know the future. We also don't know our own strengths until we are tested to the fullest. We didn't know ours. It is wonderful to have them back. Of course I don't know what the future holds for us, but I will try to cherish every good day that passes. I no longer waste time and energy worrying about insignificant things and things that are out of my control. Well I almost no longer worry about insignificant things. As long are we are a family and there is peace in the household I will always be thankful. The past seems like a nightmare and the sun is shining in the present. I still do not wish to know the future because then I would just destroy the shining sun of the present.

I have to force myself to remember the sun because of all the turmoil in the past years I am having trouble accepting the calm. I always have this feeling that something terrible is about to happen. I guess that is from having so many disappointments and trauma going on all at once, the calmness is scary. I know I have to try to live for the moment and not in the past and I do try, although sometimes it is very difficult. I have to work on being happy without guilt, even though I love to laugh and be happy and enjoy all that life has to offer. I think that at any moment the bottom may fall out and life will throw me some more curves. Oh well, if that happens we will deal with it as always. We are a strong family. I guess I never knew how strong, but I thank god for the those strong family ties in my past.

People are always so quick to judge and give advice. I have learned that there is no one thing anyone can do to stop certain things from happening. We all do the best we can do and hope for the best. I have seen children from wealthy and poor, loved and unloved families and they all make mistakes. We make mistakes. How can we judge or give advice, how do we really know what works when it comes to raising our children? How do I know that if Mr. and Mrs. X, who have grown adult children that have never gotten into trouble, would have raised Gary for instance, that he would not have make the same choices? I don't know that.

I do know that we have to be given the strength to deal with whatever comes our way. I thank God for that.

Speaking for my family. we have all grown to be different people than we were previously, at least I hope so and I hope it last forever. We are all so much more compassionate of what a life threatening illness can do to a family. What about just saying "my children are recovering drug addicts." I still can't say it out loud. Going to drug education classes, that I was forced to before each visit to the drug farm, has opened my eyes. Not that I could have or would have done anything different, but to understand that every person there had a loved one and we all shared the same feelings, hurt and disappointment, but most of all unconditional love.

The educators would lecture a lot on prevention, which in the case of my family and many others it did not apply. Many of us felt that we did every thing that they were saying to do. I believe that some people have very addictive personalities and they are at much more of a risk than others. Most people have an addiction to something or other, whether it is alcohol, drugs, shopping, eating, cleaning, working , etc.

I meet other parents and we all wanted the same things for our family members. We wanted them to be drug or alcohol free happy, responsible and productive.

I would hear cases where even after all the intensive time spent in this drug farm, which was "boot camp" (and definitely not easy). They would relapse or run during the time they had to spend at a halfway house. That was really scary, to think they worked so hard in this program to graduate and then they would return to old ways.

On Saturdays at visitation, I had become very close with one mother in particular. We would try to sit together during the meeting and visit time with the girls. I had become very fond of both the mother and daughter. I saw a mother that loved her daughter so much and I saw a very young daughter that loved her mother so much. She would have a hard road ahead, she was only 20 years old and had a very active past and a lot of hurdles to cross in her recovery. She had done it all for many years and she was only 20. Her mother actually said the time spent with her at visitation was some of the best she had ever spent with her, as there was some sort of problem since childhood. Seeing her in this environment and as a drug, alcohol free person gave her so much encouragement. We all grew to love this young girl an saw the person that was buried deep inside, hidden under all the alcohol and drug abuse. I know she had won a special place in my heart.

We keep in touch with them both. Well things, so far have not worked out so well for them. She relapsed while still at halfway and then ran before her time was up. What heartbreak! What fear!

What disappointment! These are some of the feelings that her mother had to face. She is again in rehab and I pray she follows through with the program and gets well.

It makes me sit back again and count my blessings. Whether this calmness last a year or forever, we are very fortunate. I have talked to many people who have lost loved ones to drug addiction. I often wonder why we were spared that tragedy, what purpose do we have here on this earth. Or what is in the future? I will try not to go there and for now live for the moment. I have lost my husband and the children have lost their father at a much younger age than I lost my father. However, we do have our family healthy and alive. We are more supportive of one another because of the past. Our love of family has grown and when all is said and done that is what remains important. Without the Devine Intervention would I have a family today?

What about the meeting of Tony the Pilot who mailed me the ticket when I had no money?

What about the raindrops on the awning the night I prayed for Gary?

What about the transplant?

What about the broken spindle?

What about Whitey's upside down experience the day he went into a coma?

What about Gary's sight returning?

What about Rae, doing her 'houses' at the farm on the day of her father's death?

What about the very short rain at the cemetery on the day of the funeral?

I guess I could go on and on, but I just wonder. Why?

Do you have doubts?

The End of a
New Beginning

Let's try and have faith.

Let's try and listen.

Let's try and believe we are where we are meant to be for a reason.

Let's try to understand.

Let's try and love unconditionally.

Let's try and not judge.

Let's try and smile.

Let's try and keep the sun shining.

www.ingramcontent.com/pod-product-compliance
Lightning Source LLC
Chambersburg PA
CBHW020312290526
45784CB00003B/1490